THE GOSPEL ACCORDING TO THE SAMARITAN WOMAN: A STUDY IN JOHN 4

by

Barbara Graham Tucker

Table of Contents

Introduction

Please read; it will explain some things!

This book is about a man, a woman, and a dialogue in the Bible that most people misunderstand.

If you have been a Christian long, you have probably heard at least one sermon or lesson on John 4. I have heard many and will probably hear others. However, the depth, variety, and richness of the text often lead speakers to use parts of the whole to make a point rather than let the text speak fully for itself.

I've heard sermons that present John 4 as the way to witness and present the gospel. I've heard sermons that present the woman as either a promiscuous young woman or a theological scholar. I've heard sermons on the prejudice inherent in the disciples' behavior and how Jesus is reprimanding it.

All of these have a foothold in the text, but in this short book I want us to explore John 4 in terms of context, character, conversation, conversion, and consequences. Even more, I want us to uncover how the gospel is living in Jesus' words to this woman and thus how the gospel lives for us today.

Before I go any further, I'm going to give "the Samaritan woman" a name. I'm going to call her Saahira, which you can pronounce as Su HI ruh. Why this one? To be honest, I went to a website for women's names of Middle Eastern origin and learned this one means, "earth, moon, or spring which flows constantly." Since this woman met Jesus because she was gathering physical water and since He promised her "a fountain of water springing up into everlasting life" (4:14), "a spring which flows constantly" seems appropriate for a name. Also, it sounds pleasant.

As we make this exploration, this journey, it is important that you journal or at least jot down your answers to the Selah questions, that you check out the links, and that you challenge your own thinking and attitudes. Saahira's story and encounter with Jesus is unique to her, just as everyone's encounter with Him is unique, yet Jesus reveals eternal truths as He meets her deepest spiritual needs. That is an underlying theme: Jesus tells us the truth about ourselves, about God, and about our condition, even when we dismiss, dislike, or debate it. He always tells the truth; at the same time, He does it for our salvation and transformation, not just our awareness. He tells us the truth we need in our deepest hearts.

A few notes of explanation: First, I'll forgo footnotes or involved in-text citations, because they can disrupt the reading, but I'll make it clear where I got my information. There's a bibliography at the end. Second, I will use a variety of translations for two reasons: to be inclusive (since I know my readers are using a variety of translations themselves) and to comply with copyright rules (I'm not supposed to use too much of one translation or version without permission).

Third, tenses. Yes, verb tenses. I have opted for a method that keeps everything, whether said or done, in the past tense. Usually an action or speech is treated as present tense if it is in a text under discussion. This may seem like an odd thing to note, but from an editorial point of view it matters. It keeps the writing consistent, it reminds the reader these events actually happened in the past rather than only as words in a text, and it helps me be logical.

Finally, although this book has six chapters, that does not mean you have to keep the study to six weeks. Chapters 1, 4, and 5 can be separated into two weeks if more time is needed or a chapter seems too long or complex for one meeting. Related to this point, I try to respect the reader as someone who wans to do some serious study of the New Testament; at the same time, I hope my style is informal enough and my examples applicable enough that you are engaged rather than put off.

If you are not currently a Christian believer, thank you for taking up this book and delving into Saahira's life and situation. Two thousand years has changed some of how women live in this world, but not as much as we would like to think. In many parts of our planet, Saahira's life is more 21st century than we blessed, free, and sometimes unaware Americans might realize.

If you are a Christian believer, thank you also for choosing this study from the thousands that are in print. I'm not a household (or social media) name as are some Bible teachers, but I have a mission to speak God's truth in love to an audience. I previously wrote *The Gospel According to Lazarus*, which investigates John 11. I hope you will consider that one, too. Long-term, I plan to explore the gospel themes in the accounts of Philemon and Onesimus, John Mark, and Habakkuk.

I hope you will study this book with friends or a discipleship group; sharing insights with others will help. I'm going to assume, since I'm a woman and since the main character in this study is a woman, that the vast majority of readers will be women. Women share, in general, more freely in groups than men do. (Notice, I said, "in general," not always! I can cite lots of studies from the social sciences, but we pretty much know that from experience.)

I hope digging into how Saahira converses with Jesus will reveal how we too might parry with Jesus rather than listen fully to Him. I hope that her background of shame will rend some hearts: hearts that need to have compassion for women with so-called "pasts," and hearts that know first-hand how she was denigrated in her community and culture.

And I hope we see how He desires us to transcend our cultural pride and to drink freely of living water, to worship Him in spirit and truth, and to be so excited we forget our water pots.

Sincerely,

Barbara

Chapter 1: Context

Early in my Christian life I was introduced to the inductive Bible study method, which was popularized by Oleta Wald's book, published first in 1975, *The Joy of Discovery in Bible Study*. It is a mainstay and I will utilize its processes later, since there is no reasonable way to look at a Scripture text outside of the inductive method. However, we'll start this study from the other direction. The inductive method emphasizes jumping into the text and immersing oneself in it, noting words (their definitions, origins, etc.) and their relationship to each other (grammar and syntax, two scary words for some of us).

Instead, we'll start with context, remembering that "con" means "with." We are looking at what *goes along with, around, under, and beside* the text. I like to think of the context of a passage in terms of concentric circles, widening out: the chapter of the Biblical book, the Biblical book itself (in this case, John's Gospel, the fourth one), the author's "world view," the time period and culture, the Testament, and the whole Bible. We'll shuffle that a little and start with the author and his book, then the culture and history, and last the chronology of Jesus ministry and where He is at the point of time in John 4.

Keep in mind this is a six- to eight-week study. Much lies beneath the surface here; please examine the Bibliography at the end for ways to go under the surface.

The Person of John

John, the author, did not mention his own name in the book. He didn't write, "John, the brother of James, one of the Sons of Thunder and one of the twelve disciples, who worked with Peter a great deal in the book of Acts and became a pastor in Ephesus, is penning this." John gave clues in other ways without stating his own name. He called himself the disciple "whom Jesus loved" more than once (13:23, 20:2, 21:7, 21:20). In some cases he called himself "the other disciple." He may appear as one of the two disciples in John 1:37 who decided to leave following John the Baptist and go after Jesus.

Why John kept such a low, anonymous profile is not immediately clear. However, his readers at the time would not have had any trouble identifying him. He was apparently very young during Jesus' time on earth, just a teenager, because he was still alive at the end of the first century. Scholars date his writing of the gospel at least 80 A.D., or later, and he would have been one of the remaining living apostles, or the only one by that time. Since the three other gospels had long before been written and circulated, his identity as an Apostle, one the "Twelve," would have been widely known.

John's methods of referring to himself play into the uniqueness of His gospel, which we'll discuss later. It doesn't take a beginning reader long to realize that how John laid out the life and mission of Jesus was very different from the ways that Mark, Matthew, and Luke did. Their three accounts are referred to as the "Synoptic Gospels." "Synoptic" combines two Greek word parts: "syn-" (together, as in synagogue or synthesis) and "optic (vision); in a sense, "a common view." The similarities in Matthew, Luke, and Mark (although there are some major differences) have made scholars see them as "taking a common view" of Jesus life and teachings

Based on how he referred to himself and how he structured his story of Jesus, it's easy to see John as a unique individual. But despite being "the disciple whom Jesus loved," John was probably not a meek and mild individual in his young years. He and his brother James are introduced in Mark 3:17 in this way (the context being the naming of the original twelve disciples):

> James the *son* of Zebedee and John the brother of James, (to whom He gave the name Boanerges, that is, "Sons of Thunder"); (English Standard Version)

So, why "Sons of Thunder"? Well, how about this in Luke 9:51-56:

Now it came to pass, when the time had come for Him to be received up, that He steadfastly set His face to go to Jerusalem, and sent messengers before His face. And as they went, they entered a village of the Samaritans, to prepare for Him. But they did not receive Him, because His face was *set* for the journey to Jerusalem. And when His disciples James and John saw *this,* they said, "Lord, do You want us to command fire to come down from heaven and consume them, just as Elijah did?"

But He turned and rebuked them, and said, "You do not know what manner of spirit you are of. For the Son of Man did not come to destroy men's lives but to save *them.*" And they went to another village. (New King James Version)

Fortunately, by the time the apostles led the church after Pentecost, John had outgrown some of his vengeance and bad temper. He learned to work with Peter, who tried to pick a fight about John while the disciples ate breakfast by the sea with their Lord after the resurrection (John 21:20-23). By the time he wrote the gospel, John, elderly, was a leader of the church in Ephesus and well respected. He had a long view. His desire to judge Samaritans and his struggle to understand the conversion of Gentiles (Acts 15 and Galatians 2) were long past; at the time of writing the gospel, he served in a multi-cultural church, would soon experience vicious persecution at the hands of Emperor Domitian, and would live to know the saints who took the church into the second century, such as Polycarp.

From other passages in the Synoptic Gospels, we know that John lived as a fisherman on the Sea of Galilee (also referred to as Sea of Tiberius); saw Jesus transfigured (which he alluded to in his letters later); was with Mary, Jesus' mother, at the foot of the cross and given the responsibility to take care of her; was one of the first witnesses to the empty tomb on resurrection morning; and was one of the three disciples closest to Jesus. John emphasized multiple times in his gospel that he was an eyewitness, which scholars see as "internal evidence" that the writer truly was John. Being an eyewitness was a major reason why the early church accepted books of the New Testament as inspired and part of the "canon."

John's Gospel

While John did not identify himself by name, he did identity his purpose, clearly and with no room for error. He ended the gospel with these words:

> And truly Jesus did many other signs in the presence of His disciples, which are not written in this book; but these are written that you may believe that Jesus is the Christ, the Son of God, and that believing you may have life in His name (John 20:30-31, New King James Version)

However, this was not the first time he stated his agenda; see John 19:35. While the Synoptic Gospels seem to be telling a narrative with dialogues and letting the reader decide what to make of it, John wrote with no doubt that he expected a faith response. He chose his materials accordingly, leaving out events that Matthew, Mark, and Luke include and including events to which they did not even allude.

There is considerable overlap with the four gospels, of course, as there would have to be. All of them tell of miracles, specifically the feeding the 5000 plus; all of them give details of the cross and resurrection; all of them contain seeds of what the church is to be. And notice I say, "the Synoptic Gospels seem..." Luke is pretty upfront in 1:1-4 about what he's doing, but he phrases it as a way to confirm the facts for a friend or student, Theophilus.

We know John had a clear purpose and design, but why? What about his time and place made him write, when there were already three other accounts available to the early church? That is a much, much bigger story that touches on his background as a Jew, events in Jerusalem, and long-standing prophecies.

Historical context

The Christian church began on the Pentecost (the festival celebrated fifty days after Passover) following Jesus' death and resurrection. The year? Between 30-36 AD is the date you will find on Internet sources. Earlier in that period, rather than later, seems to be supported by scholarship. The way this is figured is deduction and addition. John the Baptist began his ministry in 26 AD, based on Luke 3:1, which situates John the Baptist's ministry within the reign of Tiberius. If Jesus started a year or two later and ministered for three and a half years, that would put His death at 30 AD or up to three years later. (Scholars figure the three-and-a-half-years figure for His ministry based on the number of times in the gospel Jesus went to Jerusalem for Passover and other festivals.) Pontius Pilate was governor from 26-36 AD. The Bible writers at the time were writing to people who would have known the dates.

So, John wrote about 50 years after the events. His first readers, mostly Gentiles, did not know a great deal about the customs of Jews in Judea at that time. John himself lived in Ephesus in Asia Minor (modern-day Turkey), and the church by that time had become more Gentile than Jewish. There are specific reasons for this change in the composition of the church. One of the main ones is the destruction of the temple in 70 AD.

Why was the temple destroyed? Starting in 66 AD, Jewish partisans began organized rebellions against Rome for various reasons. Barry Strauss explained the Roman perspective in *Ten Caesars*:

> Judea had simmered for decades under oppressive Roman rule, with its high taxes and customs duties, an army garrisoned in Jerusalem, and favoritism toward the non-Jewish communities in the land. Various Roman insults to the Temple in Jerusalem created the impression of Rome as a Kingdom of arrogance." Poor Jews resented the pro-Roman Jewish upper classes, and they had more than one Robin Hood waiting for his moment. (p. 116-117)

Strauss goes on to explain that the notorious Nero, enemy of Christians, appointed the father-son team of Vespasian and Titus to high military positions and to deal with this Middle-Eastern trouble. Eventually Vespasian became the emperor in 69 AD, as did his son after him in 79 AD. From the Jewish perspective, they were revolting against high taxation and oppression. An article on *Christianity Today's* history webpage tells the story succinctly for the layman. It starts:

> Gessius Florus loved money and hated Jews. As Roman procurator, he ruled Judea, caring little for their religious sensibilities. When tax revenues were low, he seized silver from the temple. As the uproar against him grew, in A.D. 66, he sent troops into Jerusalem who massacred 3,600 citizens. Florus's action touched off an explosive rebellion—the First Jewish Revolt—that had been sizzling for some time.
> (From https://www.christianitytoday.com/history/ issues/issue-28/ad-70-titus-destroys-jerusalem.html)

Intrigues in Rome entered into the story; by 70 A.D. Nero was sending troops into Judea to put down the rebellion, which had seen Jewish victories and crushing losses to the Romans, showing how serious and willing to fight were the Jewish patriots. Nero committed suicide; Vespasian maneuvered to become emperor; Vespasian sent his son Titus to deal with the Jews, leading to a horrific siege and mass starvation. *Encyclopedia Britannica* summarizes the rest of the story:

> By August 70 CE the Romans had breached the final defenses and massacred much of the remaining population. They also destroyed the Second Temple. The Western Wall, the only extant trace of the Second Temple, remains a site of prayer and pilgrimage. The loss of the Temple for a second time is still mourned by Jews during

the fast of Tisha be-Av. Rome celebrated the fall of Jerusalem by erecting the triumphal Arch of Titus. (from https://www.britannica.com/event/Siege-of-Jerusalem-70#ref1259960)

In 2001 I had the privilege to travel to Italy and of course tour Rome. The Arch of Titus is a landmark tourists are expected to visit, although many probably do not understand its significance to Christian history or Jewish culture. However, one family I saw did. A Hassidic man was taking the photograph of his young son, about ten, outside the Arch. The little boy was wearing the same black clothing, wide-brimmed hat, and ear curls of his father's tradition. Inside the arch is depicted the Roman army carrying off a menorah (seven-branched candlestick), the table for shewbread, and sacred trumpets from the temple. To a person aware of how pivotal this event was for Christian history, it was a chilling sight.

But why was the destruction of the temple important for Christians, who did not worship there? Because it signaled a further separation of the Jewish Christians from their non-Christian Jewish brothers, and from the Jewish worldview on which much of the Jesus faith had been based. Even more, Jesus' prediction that the temple would be totally demolished, recorded in Matthew 24:2 (Mark 13:2), now had come true. The Christian History Institute's website contains an article that provides this further explanation:

But the fall of Jerusalem and the burning of the Temple in AD 70 . . . was a catastrophe with almost unparalleled consequences for Jews, Christians, and, indeed, all of subsequent history. It compelled a whole new vector for synagogue (not Temple) Judaism, it submerged the Jewish homeland for the next 19 centuries under foreign domination, it helped foster the split between church and synagogue, and it set the stage for rampant prophetic speculation about the End Times that continues to the present day. Few episodes in history have had that sort of

impact. (From https://christianhistoryinstitute.org/
magazine/article/not-one-stone-left-upon-another)

No Christians are recorded in history as having died in
the siege and attack because they had fled the city; one of the
reasons was the martyrdom of James, Jesus half-brother and a
leader of the Jerusalem church. James was stoned at the hands of
the Sanhedrin, not executed by the Romans. This act would have
motivated most of the struggling Jewish-Christian community to
migrate to other parts of the empire. Also, historical sources of
the time have it that an oracle warned them to flee.

All of these factors led to changes in Judaism and the
church that meant even more separation than we read about in
Acts 15 and in Paul's writing. And John wrote about a decade
later. Often John added a note such as "this is the custom of the
Jews" or in the case of John 4, "for the Jews have no dealings with
the Samaritans" because his readers, unlike Matthew's, would
not necessarily know these details of their culture.

These asides in John, and the way he used the term "the
Jews" have led some scholars to accuse John of anti-Semitism
even though he himself was a Jew. I discussed this in the
previous book in this series, *The Gospel According to Lazarus*.
John used "the Jews," for example in John 11, to mean the
townspeople of Bethany, the people living in Judea, the
traditional culture, the enemies of Jesus, and the leaders of the
temple. Some of his references are accusatory.

Most of the references to "the Jews" are general and have
no negative meaning attached. From a purely psychological
perspective, the leaders who crucified teenaged John's dear
friend probably earned his lifelong distrust. By the time John is
writing as an elderly man, he has seen a great deal of animosity
between the Jewish leaders toward his Christian brethren.

In summary, when looking at historical context, we
always face the question, why is John's gospel so different from
the other three? First, because of these historical incidents
described so far, which had not taken place when Mark,
Matthew, and Luke wrote their gospels, in that order in 50-60 or

so AD. Some place Mark even earlier, since his is commonly seen as the first composed gospel. Second, John was the beloved disciple with a unique perspective.

Third, John wrote to a different audience in a different time, and last, John arranged the narratives and discourses (speeches, dialogues) in his book in a way that is more about the purpose than the chronology. In fact, many question how much "in time order" John's gospel is, since it records the cleansing of the temple (chapter 2) at the beginning of Jesus' ministry while the Synoptic Gospels put it at the end and as a reason for the plot to kill Him. It is reasonable to conclude Jesus threw the moneychangers out twice. The first time was part of the reason for His trip to Galilee recorded here in John 4. In John, the act of raising Lazarus, recorded in Chapter 11, was also given as the catalyst for the plot to execute Jesus.

Immediate Context of John 4: Where Jesus is Going and Why

One of the best Bible study sources is a harmony of the gospels, which of course now you can find online. The chart on page 21 is a "partial" harmony involving John 4.

Although this harmony is not as detailed as some are, it does show that the Galilean ministry, which Matthew, Mark, and Luke recount at length, does not appear very much in John's gospel. However, it also shows that Jesus encounter with Saahira, our Samaritan woman, took place before the Galilean ministry and after His first ministry trip to Jerusalem. We might miss the timing of John 4 without this comparison of the texts.

Consequently, we see that Jesus' encounter with Saahira took place before most of His miracles, the Sermon on the Mount, and many other pivotal events recorded in the Synoptic Gospels. To take the point further, He had this conversation with a Gentile before fully reaching out to the Jews of His region in Galilee. Think about that. There is also a note in John 4:1-3:

Now when Jesus learned that the Pharisees had heard that Jesus was making and baptizing more disciples than

John [2] (although Jesus himself did not baptize, but only his disciples), [3] he left Judea and departed again for Galilee. (English Standard Version)

In other words, Jesus left for Galilee due to opposition from the Pharisees, choosing to go through Samaria. Jesus was gaining a following, and opposition was growing, but it wasn't time for the opposition to come to its climax, His crucifixion.

Conclusion

This chapter has tried, without "getting too much into the weeds" to explain what was going on in time when Jesus met Saahira. The next chapter will take the ground level view of what culturally is going on that day. The two, history and culture, cannot be easily separated, but in this case the cultural will be very personal for the people involved in this encounter.

Harmony of Gospel Texts

Event	Matthew	Mark	Luke	John
John the Baptist's ministry starts	3:1-12	1:1-8	3:1-20	
Jesus baptized in the Jordan	3:13-19	1:9-11	3:21-23	
Jesus tempted in Wilderness	4:1-11	1:12-13	4:1-13	
John speaks to a group from the Sanhedrin about his and Jesus' ministries				1:19-35
First disciples				1:35-51
First miracle at Cana				2:1-12
First cleansing of Temple				2:13-25
Meeting with Nicodemus				3:1-21
Jesus leaves Jerusalem for Galilee	4:12			4:1-3
Meeting the Samaritan woman in Sychar				**4:3-42**
Arriving in Galilee and starting Galilean ministry	4:12	1:14-15	4:14-15	4:43-45
Galilean ministry	4:12-9:9	1:14-2:22	4:14-9:62	4:46-54 (only one event recorded by John, the healing of an official's son)
Miracle at Bethsaida				5:1-47 (possibly out of chronology)

Selah

How does knowing the contemporary history of when John wrote his gospel help you understand it?

Why do you think John included totally different events than Matthew, Luke, and Mark did, and why did he leave some of their accounts out?

Find a harmony of the gospels online (here is a good one: http://www.lifeofchrist.com/life/harmony; for a classic with great detail, look at https://enduringword.com/ebooks/Harmony-of-the-Gospels-Robertson.pdf. Choose a particular miracle and see how it compares in different accounts, or if it is even recorded. Discuss why the gospels may or may not include the same events and teachings.

Think about what it must have been like for a teenaged young man, such as John, to be a disciple of Jesus.

Chapter 2:

The Samaritan Problem and the Woman in the Middle of It

As mentioned in the preceding chapter, John wrote to Gentiles as well as Jews. He found it important to insert short explanations of Jewish customs that bear upon the narrative he was building and upon the Gentile readers' understanding of Jesus' life and ministry. He did this frequently: John 5:16, 6:4, 7:2, 11:55, 19:31, are examples. John telegraphed the whole background between the Jews and Samaritans in 4:9:

> The Samaritan woman said to him, "How is it that you, a Jew, ask for a drink from me, a woman of Samaria?" (For Jews have no dealings with Samaritans.) (English Standard Version)

The Culture

We see the basic and longstanding animosity of the Jews toward the Samaritans in other passages of the gospel. John and his brother James wanted to call down fiery judgment on a Samaritan town (Luke 9:51-55) that rejected Jesus. In John 8:58 the Pharisees accused Jesus of being a Samaritan and having a demon—probably, in their minds, one and the same.

But Jesus would have none of their prejudice and hatred. He rebuked James and John (interestingly, John did not include this incident) for wanting to destroy the Samaritan town. His last words included a command to go evangelize Samaria after spreading the gospel in Judea. And of course the passage that comes to our minds most readily when we hear "Samaritan" is the story of the Good Samaritan. Jesus would likely have called him the "true neighbor from Samaria."

This parable —or perhaps a true incident—of the neighborly Samaritan follows the chapter in which James and

John questioned, "Do you want this town to be destroyed by fire?" That Jesus picks a despised people group to picture the essence of compassion and "neighborliness" is fraught with meaning. He meant to directly address their hatred. That Jesus spent time purposefully in Samaria is equally meaningful. From the very beginning of the Christian faith, believers have struggled with prejudice because all humans do; from the very beginning Jesus clarified that in His kingdom such things may exist in the hearts of humans, but they do not please God and are not His will.

But why the animosity between the Samaritans and Jews? Didn't they have some shared ethnic and religious background? Well, yes and no. The story started 700 years before, or perhaps even 900, before Saahira met Jesus. One doesn't have to read much of the Old Testament, especially Kings and Chronicles, before one encounters a pattern: the Israelites falling into idolatry and apostasy. Whether the slippage into false worship came from fear of their pagan neighbors or a desire to conform to them is not clear. Pick any chapter in Kings and Chronicles and you'll find the pattern. Worse, the kings and leaders encouraged idolatry rather than discouraging it.

However, the story goes back even further. Solomon, for all his glory, was not the king is father was. He taxed the people too much, which led to a rebellion after his death. Long story short, his son, Rehoboam, not the wisest ruler ever, decided to continue the oppression. The tribes of Judah, Benjamin, and Levites remained loyal to Rehoboam, but the others found their own king, Jeroboam, a military leader. Civil War, of a sort, followed. From that point on, around 922 BC, there were two kingdoms, the Northern tribes, and Judah, which included some elements of other tribes over the years. Judah occupied the southern portion of Israel, and Jerusalem and the temple were located there in Judea. Obviously, "owning" Jerusalem gave Judea an advantage religiously and culturally.

This tenuous political and cultural situation became far worse in 722 BC. As recounted in II Kings 17 in detail, Shalmeneser of Assyria captured the tribes living in the

Samarian region (Northern Kingdom) and deported them. Here are the first six verses of that chapter.

¹In the twelfth year of Ahaz king of Judah, Hoshea son of Elah became king of Israel in Samaria, and he reigned nine years. ² He did evil in the eyes of the LORD, but not like the kings of Israel who preceded him. ³ Shalmaneser king of Assyria came up to attack Hoshea, who had been Shalmaneser's vassal and had paid him tribute. ⁴ But the king of Assyria discovered that Hoshea was a traitor, for he had sent envoys to So king of Egypt, and he no longer paid tribute to the king of Assyria, as he had done year by year. Therefore Shalmaneser seized him and put him in prison. ⁵ The king of Assyria invaded the entire land, marched against Samaria and laid siege to it for three years. ⁶ In the ninth year of Hoshea, the king of Assyria captured Samaria and deported the Israelites to Assyria. He settled them in Halah, in Gozan on the Habor River and in the towns of the Medes. (New International Version)

The remainder of Chapter 17 recounts fully the reasons for the siege and conquest, and then the results. While the Israelites were captured and taken away to the Assyrian towns, other ethnicities were brought in to settle the former Northern Kingdom under Assyrian rule. The chapter recounts that a religious syncretism resulted. Syncretism means a mixture of religious faiths. Christianity has struggled for two millennia not to be infiltrated with non-Christian faiths, sometimes successfully, sometimes not. The practices that some Christians today follow of reading their horoscopes or praying to angels are examples of syncretism. It is also seen in nations where the church is new in a formerly animistic (worshipping nature spirits) environment.

²⁵ When they [the imported ethnic groups] first lived there, they did not worship the LORD; so he sent lions among them and they killed some of the people. ²⁶ It was reported to the king of Assyria: "The people you deported

and resettled in the towns of Samaria do not know what the god of that country requires. He has sent lions among them, which are killing them off, because the people do not know what he requires." [27] Then the king of Assyria gave this order: "Have one of the priests you took captive from Samaria go back to live there and teach the people what the god of the land requires." [28] So one of the priests who had been exiled from Samaria came to live in Bethel and taught them how to worship the Lord. (New International Version)

This might have seemed like a good idea to Shalmeneser; however,

[33] They worshiped the Lord, but they also served their own gods in accordance with the customs of the nations from which they had been brought. [34] To this day they persist in their former practices.... [41] Even while these people were worshiping the Lord, they were serving their idols. To this day their children and grandchildren continue to do as their ancestors did. (New International Version)

If religious practice has changed much in 50 years in America, think how this situation would have festered for over 700 years. The differences between the Samaria and the Jews only grew. However, as the conversation between Jesus and Saahira shows, there were some similarities between the Samaritan faith and Judaism of Jesus' day. Specifically, the Samaritans accepted the first five books of the Hebrew Bible as their scriptures, but not the remainder.

Many Jews lived in Galilee, to north of Samaria, and were required to visit Jerusalem three or more times a year for festivals, so the presence of the Samaritans between the two regions caused a problem. (Alternate travel routes developed to avoid "contamination," of course.) The Samaritans also rejected the temple in Jerusalem as the prescribed place for worship.

Without getting into every detail of their differences, we can clearly see a deep disdain, an "othering" and subordinating of the Samaritans in the eyes of the Jews. In Saahira's words with Jesus, she wanted to default to these differences rather than opening her mind to a different way of thinking.

Sounds familiar, right? It is interesting that human prejudice and bigotry, whatever the reason, exhibits itself in similar ways. We judge certain people groups that have historical problems with ethnic hatred and animosity, problems that lead to horrible bloodshed—the Hutus and Tutsis in Rwanda, the Serbians and Croatians in the former Yugoslavia, the Chechens and Russians. However, we are not entirely immune. We despise violence, but we sometimes see the "other" as dirty, smelly, less than, to be avoided, not capable of understanding the superiority of our culture.

Prejudice is simple and yet complex, and people who call for us to just "let it go" either don't understand its complexity or are unaware of their own deep-seated prejudices. I believe prejudice and racial/ethnic ethnocentrism is the human condition, not to be ignored and not to be tolerated but also not to be cured with platitudes and a John Lennon song.

Yet Jesus was willing to take water from the "dirty" cup. Yes, Jesus and the disciples had walked in Middle Eastern heat and the hottest time of the day was upon them, but we can't just say, "Well, in this case, Jesus would take some liquid from wherever it came." For Jesus, the organic became strategic. He used the need for water on a hot day to create a scenario that speaks 2,000 years later.

As mentioned, many Jews of the day would use an alternate route to Galilee and avoid Samaria. "Jesus took the direct route north from Jerusalem to Galilee through Samaria, in contrast to most Jews who took the longer, indirect route east of the River Jordan through Peraea..." (from https://www.the biblejourney.org/biblejourney1/4-jesuss-journeys-around-galilee33795/jesus-passes-through-samaria/). Jesus strategically chose His route to Galilee, where He would spend several months in miracles and teaching. The Pharisees knew He was gaining more followers than John and would start to increase opposition. The de-corrupting of the temple in John 2 had gained their attention and Nicodemus' interest in this "new rabbi" now was getting more.

In practice, however, John's statement that "the Jews have no dealings with the Samaritans" cannot be taken absolutely. Usually this referred first to eating; Jews had strict eating rituals, ones that became a point of contention in the early church. But where are the disciples during this conversation? They have gone into Sychar (the well is outside of the town) to buy food. Perhaps they believed they could find a market that catered to Jewish customs; perhaps they were hungry enough to eat something "safe enough for kosher" even if it did come from Samaritan hands. In the end, despite their deep differences, the two groups had to co-mingle at times and depend on each other.

We see this animosity, of course, when Saahira responds to Jesus' request for water from her pot and hand. Paraphrasing the various translations, "How is it that you, a Jew, are asking me, a Samaritan and a woman no less, for water?" Let's be clear: we *could* argue that the Jews should have been more open to the Samaritans since their Scriptures called them to a higher ethic regarding foreigners. The Jews did not go out of their way to find some kind of racial reconciliation; to be further clear, the Samaritans didn't either. Realistically, they were all under Roman control. They were all poor, desperately so by our standards.

Saahira's question may have been out of amazement; I can equally hear a sneer in her voice behind her query. Ultimately, we don't know. While we can read deeply into the text, and there are many cues to Saahira's attitudes toward Jews ethnically and religiously, we can't assume a level of animosity that isn't there. It was as likely that her personal life pre-occupied her more than the prejudices of her community. And that is where we turn next.

The Woman

In many years as a Christian, I've heard Saahira cast in the worst of terms. At the risk of seeming as if I'm trying to rehabilitate her image, I'd like to frame Saahira differently. I heard one hell-fire-and-brimstone preacher refer to her as a prostitute years ago. There is no basis for that in John 4. Even today, when couples cohabit frequently before marriage, we still think of Saahira as an immoral woman. Yet her sexual sins are not the point of Jesus's conversation with her. He's far more concerned about her understanding of God and His plan for redemption.

(By the way, in Eastern Orthodox and Eastern Catholic tradition, this woman is given the name "Photina." Like our words "photosynthesis" and "photography," Photina means "light" or "luminous one," and these traditions venerate her as a saint. However, since "water" is the overriding metaphor in this chapter, I am going to stick with Saahira.)

Why is Saahira treated so badly in these sermons? Because of this passage:

> [16] Jesus said to her, "Go, call your husband, and come here." [17] The woman answered him, "I have no husband." Jesus said to her, "You are right in saying, 'I have no husband'; [18] for you have had five husbands, and the one you now have is not your husband. What you have said is true." [19] The woman said to him, "Sir, I perceive that you are a prophet. [20] Our fathers worshiped on this mountain, but you say that in Jerusalem is the place where people ought to worship."

Notice that Jesus doesn't say anything else about her marital status after "What you say is true." He doesn't condemn or preach. He doesn't have to. Saahira knows she has violated the standards of her community and religion; she knows she's been isolated and ostracized by her neighbors. But let's dig a little deeper. She is feeling shame for her current situation, but her five marriages were not necessarily due to her promiscuity. Jewish women at that time did not instigate divorce, unless in situations where their families might have intervened in an unfair or cruel marriage.

If Jewish women had no such rights, a Samaritan woman's position would have been even worse. Saahira has been the recipient, the victim, of divorce five times. Why? Probably because of barrenness or some other defect. We do not know Saahira's age. She could be twenty-five, thirty-five, or past what was considered middle age. As a woman she cannot get a job and support herself; she needs protection, and it has been denied her. Of course, perhaps Saahira had been an adulterer, but adultery carried brutal penalties, although not always carried out. For some reason, she'd been passed to five men, all of whom either died or rejected her. Maybe after the fifth one she said to herself, "Who cares, at this point? I've gone as low as I can; I might as well do what I want as far as men are concerned."

And now, needing a shelter and a home, despite her reputation for losing husbands, she is living with a man without the community's sanction or witness to the event. Today, even in the marriage ceremony, we betray our deep Western individualism in relationships. We ask people to watch us make our individual commitment and celebrate it; we don't ask our wedding witnesses to approve of it and our choice of each other. In Saahira's time, the community approval was everything, and she had, for whatever reason, by-passed it.

Therefore, I wish to recast Saahira not as a rebellious sinner, a woman of extreme sexual appetites, or one who uses her sexuality for money. Instead, I wish us to see her as a person, like all of us, who is a mix of sinful desires, ways of justifying and covering our sins to the world, attempts to get by and survive the best we can, and deep personal need. In other words, she is complex—just like every single person on the planet and you, reading this book—and in the midst of a complex conversation with this stranger from Judea.

Lest you think I'm trying to recast her totally as a victim, notice her response to Jesus' pronouncement of her marital status. She changes the subject. "I perceive you are a prophet. Our fathers had this kind of religious practice . . ." In other words, "you know something, I buy that, but I have my religion, I'm okay, this is what we do here. Even though you are a Jew, and have your own way of doing things you all think is better, we're okay." Changing the subject and deflecting it to tradition was a quick form of denial.

More on that later. What I do want to emphasize is the power of shame. Saahira knew shame. She knew guilt for her current relationship, where she lived outside the bounds of sanctioned marriage, perhaps even as a mistress or some type of concubine. But after all her failed relationships, she knew shame. Shame is a powerful thing, not to be confused with guilt (although we often do confuse them), but not to be seen as totally separate, either. Guilt comes from real violation of standards of rightness, of God's law. Guilt, in a sense, is objective; a person can be found guilty in a court of law, whether they feel remorse or not. The Holy Spirit convicts us of guilt and sin so we can repent and return to fellowship with God.

Shame is something else. Non-guilty people, innocent people, can experience shame. Shame relates to other people and our internalizing of sometimes good, sometimes not so good, sometimes even silly or trendy standards of behavior. People try to shame others for not recycling or for eating beef or for driving a certain brand of car or for not spaying their pet. Mommy-shame is all over the Internet and comes in a range of pretty bizarre varieties. None of these things have to do with legal standards or violating the Word of God. And shame is intensely emotional. It can unfortunately sap a lot of our strength, time, energy, and concern for more important things.

Obviously, Saahira bore guilt at some level for her past, but that guilt took a back seat to her need of God in Jesus' plan for their conversation. More, she carried a lot of shame; she felt the sense of not being what she was "supposed to be" in her community. Interestingly, she said to Jesus in verse 4: "How is that you are talking to me, a woman?" I think she even felt shame for being a woman. That is not unheard of even today, in the U.S. to some extent but more so in parts of the developing world. In some countries, women are forced to go through difficult, medically dangerous, unnecessary, and often crudely done surgeries to remind them they are less than a man and must keep their place.

It is to those who feel shame that I write. What is causing you this shame? Are you confusing shame for guilt? Are you letting fleeting, foolish, or even unchristian societal standards (about career, talents, looks, size, health, or relationships) infiltrate your mind, control your thinking, quench the Holy Spirit's work, cause spiritual defeat, sap your creative and service energy, doubt your calling, and focus on self more than God? At the same time, are you listening to the Holy Spirit call you to real repentance when it is needed?

Conclusion

John 4:1-45 contains the story of a woman, a very real person meeting a very real Savior. The protagonist is that Savior who truly saw her as a human and a woman. He saw her in the same way He saw many other women in the gospels and how He saw exiled Hagar and her unborn child in Genesis 16 and barren Hannah in I Samuel 1. God sees us as we truly, fully are and loves us to the uttermost. As Tim Keller, Pastor of Redeemer Presbyterian in New York often says, "The Gospel is this: We are more sinful and flawed in ourselves than we ever dared believe, yet at the very same time we are more loved and accepted in Jesus Christ than we ever dared hope."

Selah

John states, "The Jews have no dealings with the Samaritans." He could also have said, "The Samaritans have no dealings with the Jews." Is that a meaningful difference?

Discuss this statement: Prejudice is simple and yet complex.

Do you agree that we tend to, on first readings of John 4, to see Saahira as primarily a sexually promiscuous woman rather than in other ways?

Does knowing the background of the animosity between Jews and Samaritans help you understand this passage? How?

Chapter 3:

Want and Water

John's record of the encounter between Jesus and Saahira is straightforward, with John's characteristic explanations—you can almost hear him making these side comments by lowering his voice. We start with verses 5-10.

> So He came to a city of Samaria which is called Sychar, near the plot of ground that Jacob gave to his son Joseph. ⁶ Now Jacob's well was there. Jesus therefore, being wearied from *His* journey, sat thus by the well. It was about the sixth hour. ⁷ A woman of Samaria came to draw water. Jesus said to her, "Give Me a drink." ⁸ For His disciples had gone away into the city to buy food. ⁹ Then the woman of Samaria said to Him, "How is it that You, being a Jew, ask a drink from me, a Samaritan woman?" For Jews have no dealings with Samaritans. ¹⁰ Jesus answered and said to her, "If you knew the gift of God, and who it is who says to you, 'Give Me a drink,' you would have asked Him, and He would have given you living water." (New King James Version)

Background

Jacob and his well figure into this conversation. The book of Genesis does not mention the well specifically, but the plot of land is mentioned three times in the Old Testament. First, in Genesis 33:19, when Jacob bought the land ("a parcel") from Hamor for 100 pieces of money. The land is mentioned again when Jacob wills it to his beloved and restored son Joseph, in Genesis 48:22. The last reference to Jacob's land on which this well is dug is in Joshua 24:32, which assures us Joseph's bones were buried on that land after many years.

This is the second time Jacob is mentioned in John. Jacob is a core part of Jewish identity, although a bit of a mess in his personal life. While his birth name meant "supplanter" or "cheater," his second name, Israel, meant "prince of God"—a big difference and a testimony to what grace does for us. The first mention of Jacob in John's gospel is in 1:51, where there is a reference to the angels descending and ascending on the Son of Man.

True, it's an odd image, but one that immediately recalled to Jesus' hearers the dream vision Jacob had in Genesis 28:10-12. Jacob was in a dark, lonely place, sleeping in the desert with a rock for a pillow after being sent away by his parents for stealing his brother's birthright. His parents feared Esau, the cheated brother, would kill him. Jacob's dream of angels descending and ascending on a ladder between heaven and earth preceded a continuation of the covenant promise with Abraham and the assurance Jacob would carry on the line of his grandfather.

Jesus used the vision as a touchpoint for Nathanael, who seemed to have a sarcastic streak. Read the encounter; it shows that Jesus was ready for anybody, even a first-century wise guy. Nathanael changed his tune when Jesus revealed a little bit of knowledge about him; Jesus does not let Nathanael off the hook. "You think it's such a big matter that I saw you under the fig tree?"

[50] Jesus answered and said to him, "Because I said to you, 'I saw you under the fig tree,' do you believe? You will see greater things than these." [51] And He said to him, "Most assuredly, I say to you, hereafter you shall see heaven open, and the angels of God ascending and descending upon the Son of Man."

In short, for Nathanael, "you will see more than your ancestor Jacob did," and to Saahira, "you will have water better than Jacob gave or ever could give you." He wanted both to move beyond their understanding of spiritual truths and their entrapment in traditions.

John also wrote a side remark that Jesus sat alone at the well because the disciples had gone into the town to buy food. Depending on what scholar we read about the location of the well, it is perhaps a half a mile or a mile outside of the main town of Sychar (which might be the Old Testament Shechem). The fact that the disciples sought food in Samaria shows they weren't always that scrupulous about cleanliness and the law. These were the men who ate corn by picking it on the Sabbath. D.A Carson notes, "Dried foods were considered less defiled than others." Regardless, Jesus was alone and a woman came unaccompanied, to draw her household water.

Want

Since the sixth hour could mean noon or later in the afternoon, one wonders why Saahira battled the heat then. Some have speculated that she was too shamed or shameful to come when the other women did. Perhaps she just ran out of water and needed some more. But no one else is there, which sets the stage for a robust conversation between a lowly Samaritan woman and a Jew. And Saahira is immediately aware of their differences.

In our translations, the words that start the conversation sound, well, impolite. "Give me a drink." No "please"? No ask, just demand? Perhaps the sense is lost in translation. Perhaps we cannot perceive the nonverbal communication of Jesus' voice and face. Is Jesus disrespecting women? Or he is communicating in his typical way, directly and with authority? It is hard to know; we may sometimes want so much to learn from a text that we pull out what is not there.

If Saahira did pick up on anything in Jesus' demeanor that she didn't like, she was ready for it. "How is it that you, a Jew, asks me for a drink?" In other words, she was astonished to be approached by a Jew. Racial prejudice was not the only concern; the Jew would have considered her ceremonial impure.

Yet Saahira was not without her own prejudices or at least deeply felt emotion due to her experiences. Here was a man, and she had no real reason to trust men. She couldn't know when He asked for water what was coming, or the character of this thirsty Jew. Was her response inquisitive ("how can this be?") or provocative ("you're a Jew, so what's up? That's not how it works around here! I might be a woman and nothing to you Jews, but I know the score!")

One of the funny things about this dialogue is that we never know if she actually handed over any water! Considering the context—the heat and dryness, the kinds of roads traveled on, and the Middle Eastern social norms about hospitality—she probably should have offered this stranger water of her own will. The fact that she hesitated at all showed rudeness rather than excused her surprise. Despite her appeal to knowledge about the patriarchs, she was not like Jacob's mother, Rebekah, who rushed to water the camels and quench the thirst of Abraham's servants in Genesis.

The way she talked to Jesus showed that her treatment by men had made her immune to their claims to power. To her Jesus is a Jewish man, maybe a teacher. So what? On top of the racial/ethnic animosity, there is a world-weariness about her. Let's not judge this woman too harshly; she is bulk of humanity. We don't know what people have gone through in their pasts. In so many sermons she is maligned. Jesus did not malign her. He spoke the truth she knows about herself.

Consider Jesus' response to her possibly sarcastic come-back. "If you knew the gift of God and who I am." That's a big "if." She didn't know either of those things, but she needed to know them, and she was about to learn. Jesus spoke as forthrightly with her as she with him. "If you knew . . . you would be asking me for something more important than a cup of physical water out of this well."

And we don't know either. We so often don't know the riches we could have if we asked, if we stopped trying to meet our own spiritual needs. We sometimes don't even know we are thirsty or what the cause of our deep aches really is. Saahira did not know how needy she was; she tried to survive her circumstances in life, and she did not know there was something better. Tired and lonely and perhaps a little cynical, she still needed to get the daily water supply.

Aside from all this, Jesus used the first opportunity to turn the discussion to her spiritual need, not her sinful past. "I can give you living water." This phrase is lost on anyone who doesn't know the Old Testament well. We don't, so it sounds odd to us. So at this point we must stop and understand the metaphor and reality of "living water."

Water

In Old Testament thinking, "living water" is running water, fresh, clean, coming from a new gushing spring or down a snow-capped mountain. Or it is precious rain from heaven, which came in Israel after many dry months every year. The opposite is not "dead" water, but motionless and possibly stagnant water. In the arid Middle East, sometimes the cistern water is the only game in town; but wouldn't everyone prefer the living water? What human would rather look at infested puddles compared to a rushing stream? D.A. Carson notes (p. 216) that this well by which they sit is both a spring and a cistern (two words are used, *phrear* (cistern) and *pege*, running spring).

You can explore the concept of living waters in these verses:

Jeremiah 2:13
Jeremiah 17:13
Proverbs 18:4
Song of Solomon 4:15
Isaiah 35:5-7
Isaiah 43:19
Isaiah 44:3-4
Isaiah 58:11
Zechariah 14:8
John 7:37-39
Revelation 21:6-8

"The fountain of living water" is a name for the LORD God of Israel. Jesus used it again in John 7:38. "Whoever believes in me, as the Scripture has said, 'Out of his heart will flow rivers of living water.'" (English Standard Versions) By identifying Himself with these terms, Jesus is equating Himself with the LORD. He is also referring to Old Testament verses that say the believer will experience an internal fountain.

From these verses we see that the blessing of "living water" is not just for physical sustenance, but is symbolic of spiritual power, of the gift of the Holy Spirit in one's being. Jeremiah preached that forsaking God was forsaking the fountain of living waters. A devout Jew would recognize that "fountain of living waters" is one of God's "nicknames" in the Old Testament.

However, although "living water" sounded good to this woman, she doesn't get the reference. Just like "eternal life" is understood today by so many as "going to heaven" when it really means far more, she didn't grasp the full extent of what "living waters" meant. She took it to mean that she wouldn't have to come to the well every day. Although the idea of indoor plumbing would have been foreign to Saahira, she might have thought, "I can skip these daily trips with this heavy jug. What a relief!"

From a communication standpoint, even if Saahira didn't understand the scriptural meaning of "living waters," Jesus' use of the term challenged her. She was faced with something ambiguous and strange; she was intrigued and not reluctant to press the matter. And she continued the conversation in a somewhat more respectful tone.

> The woman said to him, "Sir, you have nothing to draw water with, and the well is deep. Where do you get that living water? [12] Are you greater than our father Jacob? He gave us the well and drank from it himself, as did his sons and his livestock." [13] Jesus said to her, "Everyone who drinks of this water will be thirsty again, [14] but whoever drinks of the water that I will give him will never be thirsty again. The water that I will give him will become in him a spring of water welling up to eternal life." [15] The woman said to him, "Sir, give me

this water, so that I will not be thirsty or have to come here to draw water." (English Standard Version)

Saahira figured out that her conversation partner was a holy man or rabbi of some sort. She changed her tone from "you're a Jew" to "Sir." But she also was still focused on the here and now and her own physical need. Perhaps this man was a miracle worker who could provide her a limitless supply, like the widow that Elijah helped with her bottomless container of meal, or Elisha with the endless supply of oil.

And for good measure, she brought up their common ancestor. As a Samaritan, the descendant of Assyrians who intermarried with Jews over 600 years before, both she and this rabbi have descended from Jacob—Israel, the Prince of God. Whether the "our father" meant "our" of the Samaritans or "our" of both Jews and Samaritans, she brought religion into the picture. "Jacob actually drank from this well--beat that! Can you give us more than that? Are you greater than Jacob?"

Even with the more respectful address, "Sir," in v. 11, she still parried words with Jesus. We can take it as sincere, as a little amused, or as defiant. What has she got to lose? Yes, for some, the gospel comes when we have nothing else to lose. For others, we have to do some losing. Even in her low social status, Saahira held on to her culture and tradition. To paraphrase: "You don't have a bucket, so you really aren't much of an expert on wells and water. So where is it coming from? Our father Jacob gave us this well thousands of years ago. It still works. That's a pretty good track record on water from a well not running dry. That's living waters in my book. So are you greater than Jacob, our common ancestor?" Saahira attributed the well to Jacob, not God, as if Jacob would have provided such a life-giving source for 2000 years by himself.

It is interesting that Jesus challenged both Saahira and Nathanael, in chapter 1, to think beyond their present mental categories. Comparing Jesus to the Jacob of the messy, duplicitous life was a puzzling matchup. Jesus got to the point: she shouldn't compare Him and what He offered her to someone who lived 2000 or more years before. "I am giving water that springs up in the receiver to eternal, everlasting life. The water is permanent, life transforming, and spiritual. It satisfies at a hidden, deep, internal level. It indwells the receiver."

Takeaways

I think our modern, Western mind seeks to pin Jesus' words down, take them apart and analyze them, but He used a holistic, Middle Eastern image. What would a person who is constantly reminded of the scarcity of water and their own thirst want more than anything else? To have their fear of thirst and drought be removed; to have a daily, reliable abundance of fresh, running, clear water; and to be finally and unalterably satisfied. What does a person who feels unloved, rejected, broken, shamed and guilty, unaccepted and unacceptable want more than anything else? For those senses, those realities to be removed.

Although Jesus promised the receiver of this water would not thirst again, that doesn't mean that one drink does it or that the effect is immediate. However, when we truly recognize the real cause of our spiritual emptiness, our true thirstiness, only Christ and His gifts will quench that. One drink at conversion doesn't finish our thirst; we must continually visit the well of Christ to be satisfied. To paraphrase verses 13-14, "You will thirst again physically from this water. My water (transformation within by the Holy Spirit) will keep you from being spiritually thirsty again. You will have something within you that will give you eternal life." The Holy Spirit within is never exhausted, never damned up.

To be honest, Jesus' words are abstract and enigmatic, even though hopeful and connected to human yearning. We need something from outside ourselves, our beings, to come in and transform. Unfortunately, some don't recognize their thirst. Many people walk around dehydrated but don't feel thirsty. A website called dripdrop.com, which is devoted to hydration and its health effects, claims that 75% of Americans are chronically dehydrated, which can lead to headaches, foggy memory, irritability, and kidney stones.

The fact that we often don't *feel* thirsty doesn't negate our severe need for water. For example, some medications cause excessive thirst, which leads to other side effects. Spiritually, we can be dehydrated to the point of "dry bones" when we refuse to find that hydration in Christ and instead look for it to be quenched some other way. We need the living water refreshment and power Christ brings even when we are not conscious of thirst for Him.

Couple this discourse with that of John 3, where proud but seeking Nicodemus heard he must be "born again." We see that John presented a Messiah who addressed the core of the individual so that we are transformed, if we allow it, to live in conformity and harmony with God and thus be satisfied.

Conclusion

Saahira was not afraid to talk to this man at the well. She didn't understand much, so Jesus made it practical. When she changed subjects, He didn't let her. He continued with her in loving persistence and did not to let her leave the well satisfied with her wrong ideas.

Selah

Ethnic animosity is a song playing in the background of this dialogue. Jesus was very clear that the gospel and other spiritual gifts He brings are for everyone. Look at Acts 1:8. How does that verse fit in here?

While Jesus' conversation is not meant as a pattern for witnessing, it does yield insights into communicating the gospel with others. What do you notice so far about the first part of this encounter? What does Jesus do and NOT do?

Examine the verses listed on pages 38 to study the use of the words "living waters."

This encounter with Saahira happens before the many miracles in Galilee and before the "gospel" events of the Jesus' death, burial, and resurrection. Yet Jesus speaks in the present tense. Reflect on what this accounts place in the "timeline" of the gospels may mean.

Chapter 4:

Worship and Wonder

A New Way

After Jesus offered Saahira eternal, transformed life, symbolized by springs of living, rushing, pristine water—not just heaven after death but a new kind of life empowered by the Holy Spirit within—she reverted the discussion back to daily existence. Jesus wanted her to see a deeper reality. Understandably, she was trapped in a little dusty town in a region between the two Jewish sections, all surrounded by conquering Romans. Jesus challenged her to think in new categories, different pattern that apply to the whole of humanity, not just the people of Samaria.

As I am writing this book, we are in the midst of the coronavirus pandemic of Spring 2020. Churches have decided to transition to "online" or "streaming" services. The college where I work, like most in the country, is suspending face-to-face instruction indefinitely. Public schools are shutting their doors; the sports world is on hold; life has slowed like the worst snowstorm ever has hit; we are largely confined to our homes. I went to a movie today and sat in an almost empty theater. (That also might have been because the movie wasn't very good!) Travel bans, virus testing in the Walmart parking lot, and continual admonitions to wash hands, avoid touch, and "social distance" are our main topics of conversation and concern.

By the time you read this book, this strange turn of events some are calling the new normal will be over, one way or the other. I can't help but think how my singular life in my small town is being affected by something that started on the other side of the globe. I was deeply involved in my work and daily issues and responsibilities and basically detached from my existence as a world citizen. Then this virus invaded our world, like movie aliens. That turn of events may have been true of you.

Like Saahira, events are turning our constrained focus to something wider that we can't ignore.

Saahira, ignorant of who sat on the well talking to her, made of Him an audacious request: "Sir, give me this water, so that I will not be thirsty or have to come here to draw water." Audacious—because she believed He could do it—but totally missing the point. It's not physical water He spoke of, anymore than the prophet did in Jeremiah 17:3: "for they have forsaken the Lord, the fountain of living water."

The Big Request

It is here that Jesus, to prod her into understanding the nature of his gift, made an abrupt request: "Go call your husband." What a sudden twist! Why did Jesus shift this way? Was it because He was getting nowhere with this uneducated woman? Because it wasn't really proper for Him to be talking to a woman, and a Samaritan one, to boot? Because the husband would explain it to her? We can't know, but I think it was to show her she was thirsty.

Spiritual thirst is not just a matter of "I'm unhappy with my circumstances." Spiritual thirst is recognizing something deeper. No doubt Saahira was aware of and dissatisfied by her low social status and failed marriages, but what was she going to do about it? There was no upward mobility for someone like her.

It has become more common for evangelicals to speak of "brokenness." Brokenness is a helpful metaphor for understanding sin, but like all metaphors it breaks down (pun intended). "Broken" does describe our inability to fix ourselves and attain acceptance with God on our own. "Broken" does describe how we do not function as God intended. Broken communicates that God's beautiful original design is marred; not destroyed, but "out of order." Like a computer, we come up with error messages when we try to perform what we are incapable of doing.

However, "broken" tends to imply something happened, was done to us, to make us broken, something outside ourselves that we are not necessarily responsible for. Biblically, sin is our responsibility as well as our condition. It is something we both chose and something we have been given by our humanness.

So in response to her request for the living water, Jesus asked to see her husband—to help her feel her thirst. Her answer is an example of the truth, but not the whole truth. "I have no husband." Present tense. And Jesus acknowledged that, although perhaps with irony. ""You are right in saying, 'I have no husband'; for you have had five husbands, and the one you now have is not your husband. What you have said is true" (4:17b-18; English Standard Version).

Put yourself in Saahira's place—it will be a good "thought experiment," but more, an experience of grace. Imagine a conversation with a stranger, and presenting some aspect of yourself to him or her; make a statement about yourself that you know is true, but at the same times hides something painful, shameful, even something the result of a sin-driven decision. It's not hard; we do it every day.

"What do I do for a living? I'm a . . ." Does that true statement hide the truth that your job is *too* important? That it is too much a source of self-worth, that you use it as an excuse to hide from other priorities, to avoid dealing with broken family relationships?

"I have two children." A true statement. But does that cover over what perhaps only God knows, estrangement from both?

"I've been married twenty years." What is not said that causes too much hurt? What is not said about the times you have been the cause of that hurt to your spouse?

"I'm a member of .... Church." Is that a name on the rolls, or a participating member of a body?

We could continue. I know sometimes my default broken position is to hide behind accomplishments, middle-class conformity, a home in the suburbs, my profession, all acceptable screens for the struggles I would want to hide.

Of course, we do not self-disclose to strangers; we know not to share our innermost selves in initial encounters or certain contexts. Those who do, well, are just weird and off-putting. However, God is no stranger. We hide nothing from God.

Confession is not about bringing sin to his notice; confession brings sin to our own full awareness to receive grace in return. GRACE is often expressed as an acronym: **G**od's **R**iches **a**t **C**hrist's **E**xpense. It could also be **G**ifts **R**eceived: **A**cceptance and **C**ompassion in **E**xcess.

When we are children, the all-knowingness of God, his omniscience, sometimes felt, well—spooky. That might be how it was presented to us; "God knows what you're doing; you can't hide from Him, even if grown-ups don't see you." We remember the Sunday School song, "Oh. be careful little feet where you go....For the Father up above is looking down in love..." As adult believers, we should see God's omniscience as a comfort; God sees us, fully, God knows us, fully, and that doesn't change His love one millimeter or microgram.

Jesus reminded Saahira that she has been through five marriages and currently lived with a man without the proper legal and religious sanction. Over the centuries commentators have allegorized this revelation. The five husbands are seen as five false gods the Samaritans had worshipped in the past. I don't think that was Jesus' purpose. This revelation to Saahira was not a revelation about her life, but about God's all knowingness of her through this stranger rabbi. Just like rejected Hagar in Genesis 16, Jesus introduced Saahira to the God of Seeing, or the God Who Sees Me, "El Roi."

Whether Saahira was comforted at this moment, she again changed the subject from her own spiritual thirst to a cultural and religious controversy.

> [19]The woman said to him, "Sir, I perceive that you are a prophet. [20] Our fathers worshiped on this mountain, but you say that in Jerusalem is the place where people ought to worship." (English Standard Version)

If this seems abrupt, let's remember how often easy it is to deflect discussions. With these words perhaps she pointed to a local outcropping or small mountain. She played the ethnicity card. "I'm a Samaritan, you're a Jew. We differ on where we are supposed to worship God." Jesus attempted to bring them together; she raised the differences.

To provide more background, D. A. Carson wrote, "About 400 BC the Samaritans erected a rival temple on Mt. Gerizim. Toward the end of the second century BC this was destroyed by John Hyrcanus, the Hasmonean ruler in Judea" (p.216). The Samaritans did not accept any more of the Old Testament than the Pentateuch and insisted on Gerizim as the site of their region's true worship.

In the back of her mind, she had to be thinking, "How does he know this about me? He's a stranger—who told him about me, an obscure woman in a little town? Maybe he's a fortuneteller—that's what a Messiah does, right?" Notice her word, "prophet." Prophets in the Old Testament were not tricksters or clairvoyants. Her choice of words showed the syncretism of her religious background, mixing pagan practices of secret knowledge with the prophetic gifts of speaking God's truth in darkness.

Now she is in too deep. If she wanted to win an argument, she should have stayed with the subject of her background; worship is Jesus' specialty, and the central theme of the encounter is about to be revealed.

What follows is not some sort of ethnocentric response from Jesus. Jesus did not dismiss her as ignorant, any less than for her being a woman, and he does not stop engaging her, or even dumb it down for her. The next few verses seem harsh on the surface, but as a Samaritan she claimed a watered down and mixed version of Judaism. She knew about a Messiah, at least she knew the name. Jesus called her back to the roots of universal salvation—the Jewish revelation.

Worship

> [21] Jesus said to her, "Woman, believe me, the hour is coming when neither on this mountain nor in Jerusalem will you worship the Father. [22] You worship what you do not know; we worship what we know, for salvation is from the Jews. [23] But the

hour is coming, and is now here, when the true worshipers will worship the Father in spirit and truth, for the Father is seeking such people to worship him. [24] God is spirit, and those who worship him must worship in spirit and truth." (New International Version

Jesus' communication style could be gentle, blunt, direct, sometimes indirect, abstract, and purposely obscure, but never insolent or cruel, never designed to put someone rudely in their place. He had presented Saahira with His knowledge about the truth of her life and how she needed what He alone could offer, the living waters promised by the Jewish prophet Jeremiah. Either she showed misunderstanding in her response—"I think you're a prophet, so let's talk about religious differences"—or an unwillingness to deal with His claims.

Jesus essentially answered that the Jews are only partially right. In the near future, the place one worships—Georgia or Jerusalem—will be irrelevant. Ability to worship God rightly will *not* be based on geography, a truth for which we can all be thankful. Pilgrimages would be necessary. As nice as it is to visit Israel and other historical sites where Biblical or church history took place, it's not a leg up spiritually. Worship is not about trips, spending money, or where you happen to live. It's about spirit and truth. He finished with the concise but profound principle of the new kingdom He was bringing, the good news He proclaimed: "God is spirit, and those who worship Him must worship in spirit and truth."

Jesus doesn't waste words. "You don't understand. But you will worship the Father." Even in this corrective statement, He promised her a hopeful future—"you *will* worship the Father; you won't be left out of this worship. You *will* understand." I think we miss that. Jesus has a foreknowledge we lack when we engage unbelievers, seekers, or skeptics, whatever name we choose. He knew she would worship aright, in time. Even in invoking the Jews as the instrument of salvation, Jesus pointed to a future where the ethnic and historic differences will not really matter any more.

"The hour is coming, and now is here." Just as the kingdom was present in the gospels because the king was present, the hour of deliverance from false worship was present here because the deliverer was present. We can change the "was" to "is." The deliverer is the Jewish Messiah; for centuries the Messiah had been prophesied and promised through the Jewish people, despite their sin and shortcomings as God's chosen. God's plan didn't change because of their disobedience, some of which Saahira, a Samaritan, experienced as the object of their animosity. The Jews were supposed to be a testimony to all peoples of God's grace and righteousness. And they did center their worship on a place. But now...

The revolutionary meaning of verses 23 and 24 are hard to fathom. In the previous discourse in John 3 Jesus informed Nicodemus that his dependence on ethnic heritage was not enough—he needed a spiritual rebirth, one promised in the prophets but only now realizable with the coming of Jesus and what He would do.

John 4's discussion with Saahira is the Gentile version of Jesus words to the devout Jew Nicodemus. "Your dependence on ethnic heritage, and your animosity, though understandable, toward the Jews, is something you must release. A different time is coming, and since I'm the one bringing it, it's really here now. God the Father desires worshippers who see beyond genetic, geographical, and cultural distinction and worship in a way that transcends that. God is looking for those who worship based on spirit and truth. That is the only way."

I have spent years diving into these verses, and haven't fathomed them yet. They challenge me in multiple ways, and I offer my thoughts here knowing they are ill formed and immature in their development as full-grown understandings of worship in spirit and truth.

1. Jesus announced a new way here. The old was over, or soon would be. What Saahira and her neighbors

understand and practice, this tribal, ethnic basis of worship, is over. The new true worshipers are not divided by such things, blood and soil, genetics and genealogy and geography. Therefore . . .

2. We worship the Father, as opposed to "our fathers," as opposed to a tribal god, as opposed to a distance impersonal force. Our object of worship is *the* Father, in all that means theologically and personally. If we are going to worship the Father God, we must repent of those place-based doctrines.

3. Like a fish in water, we rarely understand how bound we are by culture and unable to see beyond "the way we do things" as being the correct way. Worse, we get pretty defensive about it. I can provide a small personal example, as embarrassing as it is.

   Americans and Northern Europeans value punctuality to the point of a moral virtue. It is extremely hard for us to understand that a person from a less time-bound culture has a good work ethic but is not a slave to a clock. "They should get used to the way we do things here." "Why are they so backward?" We might not say it, but we think it. When we worship in spirit and truth, we recognize cultural entrap-ment and seek to ally ourselves with the truths of Scripture that transcend our immediate families' and geography's surroundings.

4. To worship in truth implies that the Word is central to worship. The Word is found in our printed Bibles, but the Word is bigger than that. Jesus is the Word, John tells us. He is also the way, the truth, and the life. When Jesus said worship is in truth, He is also said worship is in Christ. He is the center of it.

   Further, "in truth" means "real;" through Christ will be the real way to worship. Although these verses are not seen this way, they are some of the most exclusionary statements of Jesus. We don't get to worship on our own terms.

5. Worship in spirit and truth means that the physical place does not confine or contain worship. Worship is acceptable based on the who and the how, not the where. The "how" is in community, but not in a specific style of architecture.

6. Worship in spirit and truth means our spirits are involved. This does not eliminate the place of emotions, body, tongues, or minds. It means true worship is holistic—all of our being is engaged, but not without the eternal, core part of us, the part that will live on. Our spirits must be alive, revived, and regenerated by the new birth for us to worship fully.

   We have to worship in a body; that worship is in spirit neither determines what the body does or excludes the body from taking its correct stance in worship. This is a hard one; humans have excelled in finding ways to control the body in worship: kneeling, standing, sitting, crossing ourselves, wearing certain clothes, performing other rituals. None of these things is wrong; they are only beside the point of worshiping in spirit and in truth.

7. John 4:23-24 is both an exclusion and an inclusion. No one is pushed away; no one rejected from this worship. No people group, no social class gets cut off. But no one gets in on that basis either. No one lacking dependence on Christ is included. These verses are comforting and convicting; compassionate and challenging. Is my worship accepted? If in spirit and truth.

So, what does such worship look like? Does it mean no songs written after 1960? Or before 1990? Does it mean incense and Gregorian chant? Does it mean a drummer, a cello, a violin, or no instruments at all? Does it mean a hymnal or PowerPoint? Does it mean the worship leader has to dress or look a certain way? Standing these questions up next to Jesus words, "God is spirit, and those who worship him must worship in spirit and truth," we see how secondary the questions are.

An African might worship with twenty minutes of the same chanted words. Baby Boomer Christians like to make fun of "7-11" songs: seven words repeated eleven times. Why is repetition seen this way? More emotionally open Christians poke fun at the "frozen chosen" who don't lift their hands and arms in worship. We get entangled in discussions of preference and overlook the mandate: "God is spirit, and those who worship Him must worship in spirit and truth."

As I mentioned previously, I'm writing this during the coronavirus "shutdown." My church met online this week, and probably will for a while. It's admittedly weird; I feel as if I'm "laying out" of church and neglecting my duties as a Life Group teacher. I find myself breaking out in song! Moreover, we are missing real community. Modern Christians don't often greet one another with a holy kiss, but physical presence matters.

Worship in its most basic definition is to ascribe worth to God. We can do that, fortunately, in spirit and truth, alone, in my apartment, secluded from germs and infectious people, as much as in a service with 500 others. I hope this time of sequestering ourselves to avoid a pandemic will make us crave "spirit and truth" worship in a communal setting.

Conclusion

Saahira changed the subject or, in a sense, dismissed the rabbi's words twice, one bringing up her immediate need (in contrast to her deeper spiritual thirst) and bringing up her religious differences rather than admitting to her difficult history. Now she seems to be aligned with Jesus' lead in this conversation:

^{25} The woman said to him, "I know that Messiah is coming (he who is called Christ). When he comes, he will tell us all things." ^{26} Jesus said to her, "I who speak to you am he."

Whatever her understanding of Messiah as a truth teller or teacher, it was limited, but no matter. She now talked with that person. Some critics of the Bible claim Jesus did not make Messianic claims. They can only do that if they reject any recorded words in the New Testament as authentic! Here is a crystal clear claim to Messiahship. And Saahira has a choice to make.

Selah

In your own study, read some commentaries on John 4:23-24 for further understanding of Jesus' words about worship. In a small group, explore these interpretations together. Online, you can Matthew Henry's well know commentary, as well as others through BibleGateway.com.

We do not have Jesus power of omniscience so we don't get to know the real past of people we deal with. We do not have Jesus' foreknowledge of our conversation partners' spiritual needs. How do we "get around that" or address it?

Be honest: how does your cultural training and boundaries affect your thinking about "spirit and truth" in worship.

The previous prompt presents a hard question; our natural reaction is to defend our cultural and subcultural ways and question other ways. Is it possible to get over that? How?

Can you create your own acronym for GRACE? Or another spiritual concept, such as HOPE, FAITH, or LOVE?

Chapter 5

The Announcement and Aftermath

Outpouring

After Jesus gave Saahira a corrected, radical approach to worship—one based on the *Father*, not the fathers; one based on spirit and truth, not geography and mythic narratives—she had further questions to ask. If she started out sarcastic and confrontational with this man who dared to talk to her, to "dirty" Himself spiritually as a Jew talking to a Samaritan woman, now she is all in.

> [25] The woman said to him, "I know that Messiah is coming (he who is called Christ). When he comes, he will tell us all things." [26] Jesus said to her, "I who speak to you am he."

Jesus had just told her about the Father (not a father, not the Jewish or Samaritan God, but a universal Father) who expects and empowers a different kind of worship she had never heard of before. While this rabbi offered hope, he also told her that her culture's way of doing religion was wrong. So she put out a feeler: "So, what I know about Messiah, is that he's going to explain the meaning of everything . . . is that what you're doing?"

Perhaps she was changing the subject again, since the Messiah, and her understanding of Him, had not been brought up yet. "You are trying to explain everything to me, but from what I understand, only Messiah is going to do that." Or maybe she was continuing with the ethnic differences: "We Samaritans have a Messiah. He's sort of like the Jewish one, and I know a few things about him." All three options are plausible, and she continued to reach out as Jesus continued to engage her responses, whether honest, questioning, or confrontational. Jesus brought her closer and closer. Jesus won the argument; more important, He won her.

Verse 25 is the climax of the chapter. I find it very meaningful that Jesus didn't start the conversation this way. He could have said, "I'm the Messiah, so give me some water." Granted, that was not His way of communicating, but the fact that he guided the conversation this way is intriguing. He took such an inductive, dialogic, yet firm approach. He showed patience with Saahira but didn't overlook her challenges. Our pastor recently encouraged us to start conversations with "what do you believe?" rather than "This is what I believe." Then, at some point in the conversation, we can step from inward subjectivity to outward truth. Jesus' starkly claimed that, whatever her concept of the Jewish Messiah, the Samaritan Messiah, or the global Messiah, is, He is that person. And she must make a decision.

However, John, who is a better storyteller than he is given credit for, leaves us with a bit of a cliffhanger. What did she say in response to Jesus? We don't know yet in the narrative; it's "meanwhile back at the ranch." But we do know she was eternally affected. The "camera" shifts to the disciples returning from their search for food.

> [27] And at this *point* His disciples came, and they marveled that He talked with a woman; yet no one said, "What do You seek?" or, "Why are You talking with her?"[28] The woman then left her waterpot, went her way into the city, and said to the men, [29] "Come, see a Man who told me all things that I ever did. Could this be the Christ?" [30] Then they went out of the city and came to Him.[31] In the meantime His disciples urged Him, saying, "Rabbi, eat." [32] But He said to them, "I have food to eat of which you do not know." [33] Therefore the disciples said to one another, "Has anyone brought Him *anything* to eat?" [34] Jesus said to them, "My food is to do the will of Him who sent Me, and to finish His work. [35] Do you not say, 'There are still four months and *then* comes the harvest'? Behold, I say to you, lift up your eyes and look at the fields, for they are already white for harvest! [36] And he who reaps receives wages, and gathers fruit for eternal life, that both he who

sows and he who reaps may rejoice together. [37] For in this the saying is true: 'One sows and another reaps.' [38] I sent you to reap that for which you have not labored; others have labored, and you have entered into their labors." (New International Version)

This passage deserves a chapter in itself. It fits chronologically, but thematically it seems to go in a different direction. The key word is "seem;" it really does fit logically. The overall context is that Jesus reached out beyond the Jewish culture as the Messiah for all people. The Samaritans, whom his disciples dismissed and wanted judged, were like a ready-to-harvest field of crops. Just as the disciples went to buy food that someone else labored to produce, later they would reap a harvest of Samaritan believers (in Acts 8) that began here with His sowing.

In the middle of this interlude, though, we see Saahira's true response: she left her jug and ran to her neighbors, totally without shame or concern that they would reject her. "Come, see a Man who told me all things that I ever did. Could this be the Christ?" Regardless of how her fellow townspeople had treated her, her excitement about this meeting caused her to leave both her waterpot and her inhibitions as a person of low status.

Of course, her understanding was limited and her message somewhat misleading. "He told me all things that I ever did." Well, not really, at least not in this text. But it was enough for her, like Hagar, to know she was "seen." She was no scholar, but she knew her experience. So her neighbors, no matter what they thought of her, should come and "see" Him.

At this point I have to reflect that what Saahira lacked in theology she made up for in enthusiasm. In that respect she is exemplary, while illiterate and untaught. We do not have that option. We need passion, conviction, faith AND sound teaching. She basically claimed, "He knows about me—maybe He's who we've been looking for." That was an incomplete, sketchy message at best. Jesus rectified her limited sermon; He stayed with them for two days teaching. In her defense, she at least gained the attention of her townspeople. That one of the least acceptable women in the community is calling out to everyone about someone down at the well was enough for now.

The interlude with the disciples (vss. 27-38) may strike us a bit humorous. John seemed to have no trouble poking a little fun at how unaware (read, clueless) they were. Just like Saahira does not "get" the metaphorical meaning of living water, they do not "get" the spiritual meaning of the kind of food that Jesus really thrived upon and desired. They seemed to be vitally concerned about His diet, as if He suffered from low blood sugar and didn't know what was good for Himself. So He said, whether, chiding, reminding, or revealing: "I have more important things going on. I have food to eat you don't know about." What sustained him was not food, but His purpose.

Verse 27 is an interesting insight into the disciples' views of and relationship with Jesus. John wrote here in first person, as if to say, "This is what we were thinking, and no one was saying out loud, 'Jesus, what are you doing talking to this woman?'" But they were thinking it. Why didn't they say it? Maybe so she wouldn't hear it. Maybe because they knew by then that Jesus was unpredictable when it came to talking to people who needed His message. Saahira took their appearance as a cue to go tell the men of the town. And the disciples, outnumbered, may have grown nervous at this point.

Verse 30 records: "Then they [the people Saahira spoke to] went out of the city and came to Him." They chose to believe her, despite what the town may have thought of her to that point. Saahira knew she had been seen and heard. Does not the omniscient knowledge of God into our innermost hearts serve as an apologetic? She did not and could not know the big, abstract words, but he knew Jesus saw her. First, He spoke to her (recognition), he answered her questions (acknowledgement), and He showed her herself and yet did not reject her (acceptance); He instead patiently corrected her ideas when she argued with him. Pure logical argument has its place, but we come to Jesus because of need, because of recognizing our need, and because we believe He is the only one to fulfill that need.

I occasionally read spiritual biographies of former atheists and skeptics who come to faith in God or fully in Christ: Rosario Butterfield, Anthony Flew, Francis Spufford (pretty vulgar but the second chapter is wonderful), Lee Strobel, C.S. Lewis, and others. In some cases they tell of logical progressions in their thinking, and there are of course plenty of arguments for the existence of God and the superiority of Christ. For some of us, the "mind" comes first. But something in their lives made them hungry, yes, thirsty, for something else. Their emptiness overcame their pride and their public persona as a skeptic.

In Rosario Butterfield's case, it overcame her commitment to feminist ideology and LGBT issues as well as atheism or agnosticism. In some cases, the agnosticism is accompanied by an "apatheism." The person, pre-conversion, just did not care about pursuing God. They were satisfied. And something "unsatisfied" them. Another odd spiritual category is those 10% of atheists who are mad at God, whom they don't believe exists, pointing to the place of emotion and hurt and rebellion in human rejection of God.

Saahira was unsatisfied but didn't know there was a way out—another kind of spiritual journey. Now, she did, and the oppressed, outcast, five-times-divorced woman of Sychar told her neighbors with abandon.

Outcome

The narrative about Saahira ends this way:

[39] Many Samaritans from that town believed in him because of the woman's testimony, "He told me all that I ever did." [40] So when the Samaritans came to him, they asked him to stay with them, and he stayed there two days. [41] And many more believed because of his word. [42] They said to the woman, "It is no longer because of what you said that we believe, for we have heard for ourselves, and we know that this is indeed the Savior of the world." (English Standard Version)

These verses concern the response of the Samaritan villagers in Sychar to Jesus and the woman's words. The villagers asked him to stay two days. I'm not sure how the disciples felt about this. Probably quite uncomfortable, but to their credit their devotion to their rabbi was stronger than their dislike for the Samaritans.

Are their words are a veiled insult to Saahira? "We believe, but we only came because of you—we don't really believe you—a disgraced woman—we believe because of our own experience with this Messiah." While their words may be such, I don't think it helps any to get caught there. Verse 42 is very much in line with Johns' overall theme and purpose in the book: belief based on the testimony of others and the testimony of Jesus' own words and actions (miracles, death, and resurrection). These people had the opportunity to see and hear Jesus and not depend just on what she said. At least when Saahira starts to talk about Jesus to her fellow townspeople, they seem to be willing to listen to her. They didn't scoff at her, but left to go out to the well as she left her water jug.

Conclusion

The encounter here does not seem like one of those "elevator pitch" evangelistic talks we often hear about, where an unbeliever is converted immediately after a few verses. For one thing, Jesus stayed two days to teach the Sycharites before moving on. Jesus would send the disciples later to build the church, but the believers started their journey with Him that day.

The disciples could never have planned to spend two days in a dreaded, dirty Samaritan village; to see a woman be the seed of acceptance to their message there; or really, anything else that they encountered for the rest of their lives. Despite our plans, our computer models, our research and study, we cannot see the future. It is a good thing God does not allow us future sight, so that we can trust and see Him work beyond our expectations.

Selah

Reflect on the relationship and intersection between one's personal life and the testimony of God's grace in our lives. What really matters as we minister to others, especially nonbelievers?

How might the disciples have reacted if Jesus had told them as they walked near Sychar, "Oh, by the way, we'll be here two days"?

Do you know anyone who claims to be an atheist? What kinds of things do they say about God or faith or Christ, or your own life of faith? What do you think stands in the way of their faith?

Think about and discuss with group members the words of Jesus in 4:34-38. These are usually used in missionary sermons, so we tend to overlook them for daily life—"I'm not a missionary, so they don't really apply to me." But they really are not, in context, a missionary call such as Matthew 28:18-20 or Acts 1:8. What is their meaning in this context and in your application?

Chapter 6

The Gospel According to Saahira and According to Us

To this point I have attempted to explicate or exposit (fancy words for "take apart and explain meaning of") John 4:1-42. I hope you and your group of fellow learners—which encompasses all of us—have been able to see truths and applications of this passage that you have not before. I hope you've seen it more in its total context of history, geography, culture, the New Testament, and John's gospel. In some cases it might seem like a deep dive, but trust me—there is lots more to say and glean from this narrative. I recommend full studies of John such as D.A. Carson's or F.F. Bruce's, to which I am indebted as sources.

So, where does it leave us? Any conclusions or applications I make in this chapter are really just seeds for you to discuss, reflect upon, or use for further study by yourself or with others. The whole Bible is intimately intertwined; we've already seen how these 42 verses are tied to and illuminated by Genesis, II King and II Chronicles, the prophets, Luke 9, Luke 17:16 (where it is noted that one of the ten healed lepers, the one who gave thanks, was a Samaritan), Acts 1:8 and 8, and other parts of John. We should probably even read the parable of the good Samaritan neighbor differently now.

The title of this book, however, is *The Gospel According to the Samaritan Woman*. In a sense, I'm sticking my neck out to title it that; I confess it's a bit of a marketing ploy, since books in series always get more attention these days. The first book in the series, *The Gospel According to Lazarus*, explores deeply John 11 (yes, I have a great love for John's gospel). Why "the gospel" as a common word?

Our understanding of the gospel should deepen through the years. Early in our experience we are told it means "good news," coming from a Greek word *euangelion* (obviously close to "evangelism"). However, the real use of the word in Greek has wide implications, just like the word "blue" has many connotations for us today: a political party, an emotion, a kind of music, etc.

In the previous book in this series, I spent the last chapter on a word study of "gospel" using a variety of sources. Here, I will just quote two from that chapter. The meaning of "gospel" is far richer and life-changing than "good news"—that you're getting a tax refund is good news, too, but that is not the kind of good news the gospel is talking about.

First from R.C. Sproul:

> In ancient days when soldiers went out to battle, people waited breathlessly for a report from the battlefield about the outcome. Once the outcome was known, marathon runners dashed back to give the report. That is why Isaiah wrote, "How beautiful upon the mountains are the feet of him who brings good news" (Isa. 52:7). The watchman in the watchtower would look as far as the eye could see into the distance. Finally, he would see the dust moving as the runner sped back to the city to give the report of the battle. The watchmen were trained to tell by the way the runner's legs were churning whether the news was good or bad. If the runner was doing the survival shuffle, it indicated a grim report, but if his legs were flying and the dust was kicking up, that meant good news. That is the concept of gospel in its most rudimentary sense.

Saahira's feet were beautiful that day, not because she was preaching the full gospel—she couldn't know it—but because she was sharing what she knew about the Messiah who asked her for some water at the well.

The second passage I used from the book on Lazarus is from a Roman Catholic scholar who explains more of the word's history:

> The term [*euangelion*] is not necessarily indicative of something pleasant or happy. It originally referred to the

utterance of an emperor, even if the content was not particularly pleasant. For example an "evangelion" might announce an increase in taxes or the summoning of an army. In God's Word, the Gospel might include promises of salvation, offers of forgiveness, and blessings. But it might also include the teachings on the need for repentance, on the requirement to take up a cross, on accepting that we may well be hated, and on the fact that judgment is looming . . . .

The emphasis of the word "evangelion" was that it had authority behind it, authority capable of changing your life. Thus if the emperor announced that he was paving a nearby road, or raising taxes, or summoning men to arms, or declaring a holiday—whatever the message contained, you knew your life was going to change, perhaps dramatically, due to the emperor's authority. (Monsignor Charles Pope).

I use these two quotations to illustrate that our understanding of the gospel should flourish far beyond the elementary meaning that it's good news. The Apostle Paul defines the theological and historical content of the gospel in I Corinthians 15:1-10 (quoted here in the English Standard Version).

> [1]Now I would remind you, brothers, of the gospel I preached to you, which you received, in which you stand, [2] and by which you are being saved, if you hold fast to the word I preached to you—unless you believed in vain. [3] For I delivered to you as of first importance what I also received: that Christ died for our sins in accordance with the Scriptures, [4] that he was buried, that he was raised on the third day in accordance with the Scriptures, [5] and that he appeared to Cephas, then to the twelve. [6] Then he appeared to more than five hundred brothers at one time, most of whom are still alive, though some have fallen asleep. [7] Then he appeared to James, then to all the apostles. [8] Last of all, as to one untimely born, he

appeared also to me. [9] For I am the least of the apostles, unworthy to be called an apostle, because I persecuted the church of God. [10] But by the grace of God I am what I am, and his grace toward me was not in vain.

Usually we stop at verse 7 to define the gospel, but I have included 8-10 to demonstrate that the gospel does not stop at historical truths of Jesus' death, burial, and resurrection. We must understand the gospel to have personal implications as well as indisputable historical accuracy. (I recommend Gary Habermas' videos on YouTube for more study on the subject of historical proofs for the resurrection and thus gospel).

The gospel is God's means of grace to us. Saahira in our story knew only that she met the Messiah foretold since Moses' day. Her concept of the Messiah did not really fit the Jewish traditional concept or the full understanding revealed after the cross and resurrection, such as to the disciples on the road to Emmaus or to the apostles. In the two days Jesus spent with them, the Samaritan villagers received a crash course in true Messianic theology and Jesus' identity. We don't know these details; we do know that Jesus loved the Samaritans and wanted them to be among the first to join the kingdom.

Just as the twelve were probably perplexed and disturbed that Jesus wanted to travel through Samaria on the way back to Galilee, and just as they questioned why He was conversing with a woman, they probably wondered why the Samaritans held a place of priority. Interestingly, Jesus' opponents later accused him of being a Samaritan (John 8:48), as if that were the worst thing in the world to say; they also implied that He was born of adultery (John 8:41).

Yet the New Testament accounts tend to portray the Samaritans in a good light despite the culture's prejudices. Luke recorded that of the ten cleansed lepers, the only thankful one, the one who came back, was a Samaritan (Luke 17:16), and the true example of a good neighbor was not a Jew, but an enemy of Jews. Jesus purposefully exploded stereotypes in His foundational teachings on righteousness.

The gospel is not fully expressed in this encounter, because it happened before the cross and resurrection and full revelation of Jesus' purpose and identity. On the other hand, this account does teach us these aspects of the gospel.

1. The gospel transcends difference and prejudice. Notice the word "transcends," not "ignores." Racism and prejudice are sin, and the gospel does not "ignore" sin—it addresses it fully. Jesus did not, in this encounter, ignore the fact that Saahira was deeply conscious of her difference from Him; He talked about it. But He found, first, common ground through the metaphor of water and thirst, and then said, in essence, "Let's look at this from a different perspective, God's perspective, from the purposes of God in history not the animosity of men toward each other."

   At the same time, He doesn't ignore that the Jews and their message were the method through which God revealed His purposes and would bring the Messiah and salvation. This encounter teaches us that personal need can be met without weakening the seriousness of our sin or the factuality of the Bible's claims.

2. The gospel transcends one's past. Saahira is the Hagar of the New Testament. "He told me everything I ever did." Yes, an exaggeration, but Saahira, like Hagar, was seen by the God who sees, is heard by the God who hears. She is *fully* seen, not just the ugly or shameful or socially unacceptable parts. Transcending doesn't mean turning away. It means moving above and beyond it.

   Personally, I believe this is a core message of this encounter. We can understand why John included the dialogue with Nicodemus, but this woman? She was the very opposite of a righteous member of the Sanhedrin. The details about her personal life almost hit us in the face, as it affected her the same way to be told them by a stranger. She did not deny them; she tries to change the subject, but she did not say, "What are you talking about?" Saahira's story screams liberation from our mistakes, bad choices, sins, and brokenness.

3. The gospel transcends cultural religious teaching. I have been privileged in the last few years to teach English to refugees from Sudan, Iraq, and Iran. One gentleman from Iran attends our church. He is bolstered by the relationships he has made there and pulled to something in this Christianity that, if he embraces it, will mean devastating consequences to his family life. For decades—he's mid-50s or older—he has known nothing but Islam. But something, Someone, is speaking to him.

   More Muslims are converting to the Christian faith in the last ten years than in all of history, and the stories of how their dreams are the vehicles of coming to Christ fascinate and inspire. There are millions of such accounts, too many to be passed off as hearsay or fairy tales. If you are unfamiliar with this movement of God, which is all it can be and not just a sociological trend, you should look into it at reliable and even secular sources of information, such as this one: https://www.npr.org/2018/12/14/669662264/iranians-are-converting-to-evangelical-christianity-in-turkey (there are hundreds of other such articles on the Internet).

   If you know anyone who comes to Christ from a collectivistic or highly traditional culture, you know how difficult that step is. Friends of mine who are long-term missionaries in Japan say that an interested Japanese person may attend services and events held by their church for years, but never truly commit to Christ; they eventually step back away from the Christian community because of pressures from family, community, and tradition.

   What this passage in John 4 proclaims is that our faith is not a cultural faith. While our faith is expressed differently in various cultures, our faith is a global one, a universal one—it's for everyone. One of my favorite verses if Revelation 5:9:

   > And they sang a new song, saying:

   > "You are worthy to take the scroll,

And to open its seals;
For You were slain,
And have redeemed us to God by Your blood
Out of every tribe and tongue and people and
nation,

Read that last line: it is the ultimate in inclusive. No one is excluded from this plan of God, this gospel, by birth or language or culture. And if we do anything or believe anything that would imply it is—where does that leave us?

Jesus told Saahira: in the future, which is now, worship will have nothing to do with a mountain or a temple or a site or a pilgrimage. Those who worship the Father (that name in itself is revolutionary, a term for God rarely used in the First Testament) will do it in **spirit and truth**, not in a geography-based way, not in a way that excludes a culture or people group.

For myself, as I have studied these chapters and written these words, I am humbled, convicted, and disturbed by how much I have succumbed to my "whiteness," my middle-classness, my professionalism, my education, and my privileges. Ultimately, my, and I hope your, existence will be at the throne of God, singing that He is worthy to open the scroll of judgment that leads to a new heaven and earth. We will be there with the Vietnamese orphan, the African villager, the European housewife, the South American businessman, the Russian pastor with only one thing in common that matters: we have been redeemed to God by Christ's sacrifice.

Conclusion

Perhaps you are reading this book because you were invited to a group study, but you have not embraced Jesus as your Savior in fullness. What holds you back? Dean Inserra, a pastor in Florida, has written an insightful but disquieting book,

The Unsaved Christian. He pinpoints those who might take for granted that they are by default "Christians" because they look a certain way, attend a church occasionally, have family members who are believers, live morally, or have never had any connection to Islam, Judaism, or Buddhism. Pastor Inserra challenges these folks to understand the claims of Christ fully and stop assuming one's place in the family of God.

Polling organizations, such as Gallup and Pew, have in the last twenty years started using the term "Nones" to denote people who choose no religious affiliation. Since prior to that time there was no such choice other than Catholic, Protestant, Jewish, Islam, etc., poll-takers about religion had to choose what was offered. The data looks now as if there was a great increase in the number of unaffiliated persons in the U.S. That is not entirely the case, although it is true that Americans today feel more comfortable not claiming an affiliation to a church or denomination.

We can draw the conclusion that it is less likely for a person to call himself or herself a Christian now and not really embrace the faith with understanding. Still, there is an American tendency to see the word "Christian" as a social category rather than what it mean to the people as recorded in Acts 11:26: "And the disciples were first called Christians in Antioch." (Use a concordance to find out how many times the word Christian is actually used in the New Testament—it's interesting!)

Socrates said, "The unexamined life is not worth living." (and I've seen the reverse: "The unlived life is not worth examining"!) Paul took up the same theme to tell us in II Corinthians 13:5: "Examine yourselves *as to* whether you are in the faith. Test yourselves. Do you not know yourselves, that Jesus Christ is in you?"

I do not ask you to examine yourself to spread doubt; I ask it because you might have entered this Bible study at the request of a friend and are still wondering what the claims of Jesus are about. This passage in John 4 does not reveal the entirety of the gospel. There is nothing about the cross or resurrection. What is here is the grace of Jesus, His kindness, His unique character, His fulfillment of prophecy, His call to a radical kind of worship and approach to the Father. I hope in these pages you, like Saahira, have seen some of the richness of Jesus and want to know Him more.

The gospel according to Saahira, the Samaritan woman, a low-status female in a despised culture is not simply about the facts or the theology. The gospel's truth is power, as the Apostle Paul wrote in Romans 1:16: "it is the power of God that brings salvation to everyone who believes: first to the Jew, then to the Gentile." The gospel according to Saahira is the same as the gospel according to you. What gospel do you live? What good news is evident in our lives?

Selah

One of the arguments of this book is that gospel is much more than "good news that you can go to heaven when you die," although that certainly is good news. Reflect on and discuss how your understanding of the gospel has changed in your Christian experience and perhaps in this study.

Reflect on and discuss Paul's words in II Corinthians 13:5 about self-examination and your faith.

Look up other passages where Samaritans are featured in the Bible. What parallels can we draw for our society today?

In terms of self-examination, what gospel do others see in you in your everyday life?

Bibliography

F.F. Bruce. *The Gospel of John.* Eerdmans, 1983.

D.A. Carson. *The Gospel According to John: A Pillar New Testament Commentary.* Eerdmans, 1991.

A.J. Kostenberger, *A Theology of John's Gospel and Letters.* Zondervan, 2009.

B. Strauss, *Ten Caesars: Roman Emperors from Augustine to Constantine.* Simon & Schuster, 2020.

A little about the author

I came to Christ in 1971 as a middle-teenager. (So now you know my general age). That made me the first believer in my immediate family. I was fortunate to be discipled in a large church with lots of resources. Warren Wiersbe and Richard Wurmbrand spoke at the church I belonged to, so I was blessed with an introduction to the wider world of Christianity early on.

Two years later I moved over 600 miles to attend a faith-based college that no longer exists, or at least, exists under the auspices of a different college with which it merged. Many things about that now gone college were fundamental to who I am today, with any emphasis on the word, "fundamental." (Some will get my attempt at humor.) Suffice it to say that we had strict, sometimes silly, rules that were common at that time. I appreciate that the college experience made me aware that rules don't build us up in the faith but are sometimes necessary for a life of order and progression.

After college I attended graduate school for a year in another region of the country; by the age of 23 I had lived in lower mid-Atlantic, the somewhat deep South, and the sort-of Midwest. I settled back in the Southeast and there I've stayed for, oh, my goodness, 40 years! I married, and we raised our son there, and I've had a long career in higher education. The Southeast is home, despite sometimes not fully understanding aspects of the Southern experience and still feeling a bit like an outsider after four decades. I still can't call a 7-Up a "Coke" and can take or leave college football, but I like the long growing season for fresh vegetables, the politeness, and the flora and fauna.

Although my main professional role has been an instructor of English and communication in a private, community, technical, and state college (in that order), I have performed numerous jobs in college administration, everything from a debate coach to a public relations agent to an assistant vice president to a department chair. I have three graduate degrees that basically have taught me I have a lot more to learn, even in my sixties, and look forward to it. I began writing fiction seriously in the early 2000s and began publishing novels in 2008. I'm working on numbers 8 and 9 as I write this book. (Having some writer's block, actually, on the stories). I also write plays, blogs, Bible studies, academic articles, textbooks, and instructional materials.

A lifetime of experiences in teaching, research, writing, raising a child, marriage, caring for a mother in hospice, campus ministry, teaching English as a Second Language, and Bible teaching lies behind this book. Writing is my gift, when I'm not in the classroom, and writing about Scriptural truth is my passion. I hope it shows.

Enjoy,

Barbara

Other Works by Barbara G. Tucker

The Gospel According to Lazarus

Leading in a Strange Land: A Study in Daniel and Leadership

Novels

Traveling Through

Cross Road

Legacy

The Unexpected Christmas Visitors

Bringing Abundance Back

Long Lost Family

Long Lost Promise

Visit her website:

www.barbaragrahamtucker.com

and blog

partsofspeaking.blogspot.com

NOTES

NOTES

Printed in Great Britain
by Amazon